Swan Song

Swan Song

Poems of Extinction

by J. Patrick Lewis

woodcuts by

Christopher Wormell

CREATIVE EDITIONS

For Matty, best ever—with love, J.P.L.

To Mary, C.W.

Illustrations copyright © 2003 by Christopher Wormell

Text copyright © 2003 by J. Patrick Lewis

Published in 2003 by Creative Editions, 123 South Broad Street, Mankato,

MN 56001 USA. Creative Editions is an imprint of The Creative Company.

Designed by Rita Marshall.

Printed in Italy.

Library of Congress Cataloging-in-Publication Data

Lewis, J. Patrick.

Swan song / by J. Patrick Lewis; illustrated by Christopher Wormell.

Summary: Contains poems about the world's extinct animals.

ISBN 1-56846-175-5

1. Extinct animals—Juvenile poetry. 2. Extinction (Biology)—Juvenile

poetry. 3. Children's poetry, American. [1. Extinct animals—Poetry. 2. Extinction

(Biology)—Poetry. 3. American poetry.] I. Wormell, Christopher, ill. II. Title.

PS3562.E9465 S93 2003   811'.54—dc21   2002031460

First Edition

5 4 3 2 1

FOREWORD

More than ninety-nine percent of all species that have ever lived are now extinct. The most enduring and compelling image of large-scale death is that of the dinosaurs, colossal reptiles who vanished from Earth sixty-five million years ago.

At the other extreme, the last falling feather of the Passenger Pigeon, which once numbered in the billions, had all the impact of a single snowflake fluttering down a canyon. The last Barbary Lion, far from being celebrated, amused a North African king as a carpet. The howling echo of the Miss Waldron's Red Colobus monkey will soon be a memory to no one at all.

This book is about the recently departed. In Earth's great forests and fields, they buzzed and chirped and bellowed through little incidents of sorrow from roughly 1627 to 2000. Whether beautiful or homely, giant or dwarf, each species was its own drama in many disappearing acts, even if it was very far off the Broadway of the dinosaurs.

On Earth, six animal species die every hour, many of the most recent due to climate change, habitat destruction, or human greed or carelessness or indifference. Here are a few small epitaphs in verse to mark their passing.

Bos primigenius   Extinct c. 1627   Europe

THE
AUROCHS

You were as different from the cow

As, say, the wolf is from the dog,

But as your Latin name implies

Most creatures in the cattle-og

Owe you a debt of gratitude,

Grandfather of the bovine race,

Rumbling massively around

History at a bullish pace.

1627 German astronomer Johannes Kepler creates the first star catalog, noting the position of 1,005 stars. 1640 England's first stagecoach lines are established as roads are built to improve passenger travel.

THE DODO

Without an enemy to face,

    The dodo ceased to fly,

Eating fruit from off the ground.

    Centuries flew by.

Settlers came and made them game:

    The dodo ceased to be

From cats and dogs, black rats and hogs,

    And man's efficiency.

Three centuries since dodos lived,

    A tree called the Calvaria

Now faces death because no dodo

    Navigates the area.

There was a time when dodos ate

    Its seeds and passed them through.

Now seeds lie still, the dodo's gone,

    The trees are going too.

Cygnus sumnerensis   Extinct c. 1690

Chatham Island, New Zealand

Aepyornis maximus   Extinct c. 1700   Madagascar

CHATHAM ISLAND SWAN

Chatham Island, rich and rare resort

For migratory marvels on the wing,

Is something of an empty royal court:

A paradise without a queen and king.

Exotic birds were commoners to those,

Who once, an age ago, could silhouette

In symmetry an S on S, and pose,

Or glorify a shoreline, dripping wet.

But beauty is handmaiden of the strong,

Or else we might have heard

    this Swan's swan song.

THE ELEPHANT BIRD

Eggs the size of a dinosaur's,

Legs as big as a beam,

The Elephant Bird, the Elephant Bird

Was the ten-foot bird supreme.

Claws as sharp as razor blades,

Beak like a broad-head spear,

The Elephant Bird, the Elephant Bird

Had nobody else to fear.

Sixty million improbable years—

The Elephant Bird's timespan—

Till the Elephant Bird, the Elephant Bird

Met up with the likes of Man.

| 1690 | The first paper mill in America is established at Germantown in the Pennsylvania colony. | 1700 | The population of London, the largest city in Europe, climbs to a new high of 550,000. |

Britain's American colonies number 262,000 people, many of them in Boston and Philadelphia.　　1767　　English chemist Joseph Priestley creates carbonated water, which is soon used in drinks and tonics.

STELLER'S
SEA COW

Big as a mastodon, a cow

Fed for a month three dozen men.

Three dozen men it took to hook

And haul the beast to land, and when

They'd hack with knives and bayonets

Great strips of blubber, there she'd lie

Unmoving on the ice, and let

Out something like a human sigh.

Discovered, 1741,

She dwarfed all creatures of the sea,

Except the whale, so let us toast

Sea cows in their enormity.

1800

Italian physicist Alessandro Volta invents the
voltaic cell, making electric batteries possible.

The armies of French emperor Napoleon Bonaparte
cross the Pennine Alps and conquer Italy.

THE BLUE BUCK

Small herds of springbok gambol here.

    Sable, gazelle and roan

Still paint the plains of Africa—

    You disappeared . . . alone.

Blue beauty was a burden—in

    A country coated tan—

For you, a brilliant animal

    Advertisement to man.

By 1800 you'd become

    Museum skeletons,

Who could not range beyond the reach

    Of European guns.

Old sun sprawls over Africa;

    New rains that fall are few.

Once upon a time there was

    An antelope in blue.

RODRIGUEZ
GREATER SADDLEBACK
TORTOISE

Three causes led

To your eventual defeat:

Your pace;

Your innocence;

And your delicious meat.

Three reasons for

A rousing fare-thee-well:

Your pace;

Your innocence;

And your amazing shell.

THE PAINTED
VULTURE

Bog meadows, wide

    Savannahs burned.

The painted bird

    Sat unconcerned.

His dark eyes, dull

    As charcoal, peered

Into the smoke

    That finally cleared

Enough so he

    Could then partake

Of toasted lizard,

    Frog, baked snake.

But as he ate,

    How could he know

What little life

    Was left to go?

1818   *Frankenstein*, a popular novel by English author Mary Wollstonecraft Shelley, is published.   1844   Samuel Morse sends the first message by way of his new invention, the telegraph.

THE
GREAT AUK

Like bowling pins corralled in pens,

The Great Auks, dumb to danger,

Regard the hunter with a club

As uninvited stranger.

Men rake Auks to the boiling pots

For dinner. First the birds

Are cleanly plucked for eiderdown

And eaten afterwards.

Icelandic sailors find the last

Remaining Auks, a pair

Who utter no alarm, perhaps,

Too desolate to care.

EASTERN ELK
(WAPITI)

Man the hunter,   End of Elk meat,

Elk the hunted,   Teeth and pelts.

Hounded, cornered   Man goes after

And confronted.   Something else.

16   1877   The *Paraguay*, the first refrigerated ship,
hauls frozen meat from South America to France.   1881   Famed American outlaw William Bonney
("Billy the Kid") is shot after killing 21 men.

THE
QUAGGA

I was *Quahah, Quahah,* Bushman's honored name.

Wild horse, tame zebra, plains zephyr,

White-leg in solids and stripes after a fashion.

I knew Hottentots in Dreamtime.

I slaved as the Boer's nightwatchman.

I befriended ostrich, who could see horizons.

I ran with hartebeest, who could smell lion

    to the Orange River.

They raced with me, who could hear grass sigh.

I grazed long on short stubble.

I raged against cages, for all the good it did.

I lived on as purse or pouch or pocketbook.

883   The world's first skyscraper—a 10-story building—
is built in Chicago, Illinois.   1899   Coca-Cola, the carbonated drink soon to become
world famous, is bottled for the first time.   17

THE
LAUGHING
OWL

Thomas Hyatt Potts caught

the second to last Laughing Owl

without a second thought.

Her heart beating wildly,

her face calm as a hunter's moon,

she looked at the man who knew

he'd had the last laugh.

He weighed and measured her,

put her in an ether chamber to die,

skinned and stuffed her with tree

fern down, then fumigated her in

arsenic, and let her dry for all to see.

For many days, her mate returned

to the spot where she had been taken.

His grief finally spent, he swooped

down to a footnote nest of history

crying and laughing by turns.

Slaughter has reduced a bison population that
numbered 65 million in 1800 to fewer than 300.

1903   Americans Wilbur and Orville Wright make the first
manned flight in a gas-powered aircraft.

ARIZONA
JAGUAR

Description: Loner; nightfall eyes;

Coat of spots on spots (disguise);

Once the New World's largest cat;

Mountain, grassland habitat;

Fed on any kind of meat;

Stumbled down a one-way street;

Color of a jealous sun.

Status: Nowhere. *Future:* None.

THE PASSENGER PIGEON

In 1870, a flock of Passenger Pigeons a mile wide

and three hundred twenty miles long thundered over

the Midwest, abolishing the sky. Two billion birds

swirling to the cage end of oblivion.

Imagine, if you can, that once in America,

almost half the birds alive were these migrating doves.

Humans sewed their eyes shut and nailed their feet

to a stand. When other birds flew down to investigate,

nets and guns welcomed the "stool pigeons" forever.

On September 1, 1914, at exactly 1:00 p.m.,

while the world was making unforgivable war,

"Martha," a 29-year-old Passenger Pigeon, the last

of her kind, died in her sleep at the Cincinnati Zoo.

The news of her death attracted no attention—

a two-word bird in the Song Book of Forgetting.

| 1912 | The "unsinkable" British luxury liner *Titanic* sinks on her maiden voyage across the Atlantic. | 1914 | World War I begins; it will last five years and result in more than 10 million deaths. |

The Panama Canal, a manmade waterway linking
the Atlantic and Pacific Oceans, opens. 1917 Five hundred forty-three people are killed at Modane,
France, in the worst train wreck in history.

Conuropsis carolinensis carolinensis   Extinct c. 1914

Carolinas and Virginia, USA

Panthera leo leo   Extinct c. 1922   North Africa

CAROLINA PARAKEET

Lady Jane: *Here we sit, the only parrot pair in America left alive . . .*

Incas: *. . . after thirty-two years in a zoo. Too old to breed.*

Lady Jane: *Remember when we flew by the thousands?*

Incas: *Only a century ago.*

Lady Jane: *What happened, Incas?*

Incas: *We ate their grain and pears and apples.*

Lady Jane: *They destroyed our homes.*

Incas: *Everyone but Man inherits a cage.*

THE BARBARY LION

Leo Leo, picture show

Worthy of Henri Rousseau.

Leo Leo, where's the mane

That rippled pulses on the plain?

Leo Leo Golden Hair,

Dying out with Atlas Bear.

Leo Leo, perfectly

Magnificent a memory.

Ovis canadensis auduboni   Extinct c. 1925

Dakotas and Nebraska, USA

Thylacinus cynocephalus   Extinct c. 1933   Tasmania

BADLANDS (AUDUBON'S) BIGHORN SHEEP

Men arrived,

Bighorns ran

up the buttes

faster than

anyone

could have guessed.

Prairieless

and distressed,

they could not

understand

hopelessly

barren land.

What is done

won't undo.

Bighorn Sheep,

where are you?

TASMANIAN POUCHED WOLF

You were the strangest of the strange.

How did good nature rearrange

All of those unusual parts?

Kangaroo tail,

Wild dog's heart,

Tiger stripes,

Opossum's pouch,

Wolf's head

And hyena's gait—

Diversity to celebrate.

Nature need make no apology—

You belonged in Greek mythology.

Scottish inventor John Logie Baird produces
the first image on a television screen.

1933

The Great Depression covers the United States;
15 million people are out of work.

Moho nobilis Extinct c. 1934 Hawaii

Hawaiian O-O

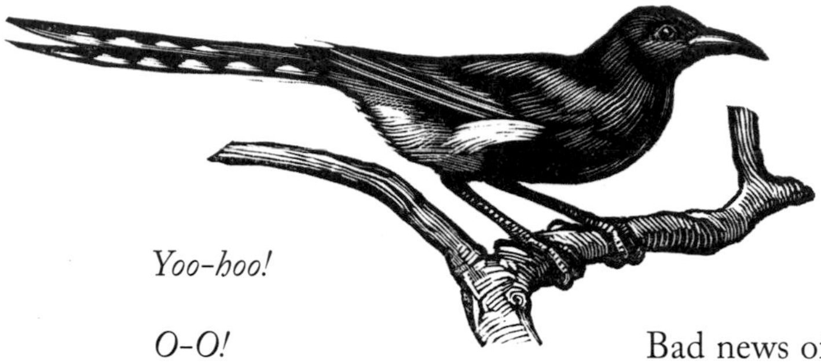

Yoo-hoo!

O-O!

You flew

So low

To say

Alo-

ha, *er*,

O-O!

Your coat,

You know,

Could steal

The show,

But that

Was oh

So long

Ago,

So long

Ago.

So long,

O-O.

Panthera tigris balica Extinct c. 1937 Bali, Indonesia

Bali Tiger

Bad news of 1937—

The Hindenburg explodes killing 35.

Amelia Earhart disappears over the Pacific.

Japan launches all-out war against China.

Hitler proclaims God his friend and ally.

And the world wept.

Newspapers buried another tragedy

In their back pages:

The last Bali Tiger, a female, is shot dead.

And the world slept.

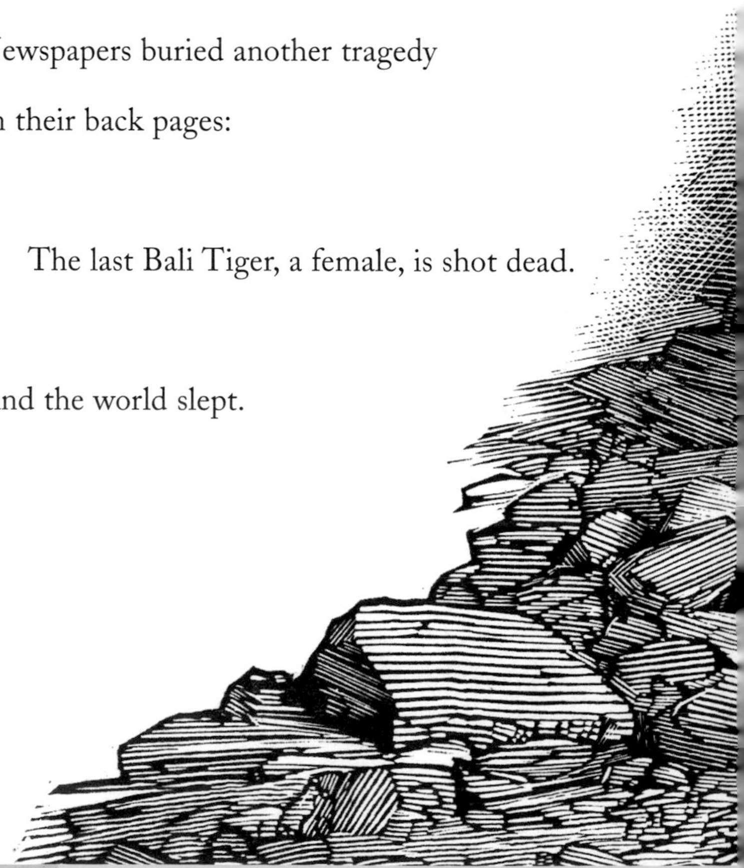

1934 To claim grasses and government bounties, American ranchers begin slaughtering wild horses.

1937 Astronomer Grote Reber builds the world's first radio telescope to listen to space.

Coregonus johannae   Extinct c. 1960   Lakes Michigan and Huron, USA and Canada

DEEPWATER CISCO

Great Lake luck's a-runnin' thick.

Cried the grinning fisherman,

Cisco barrels rolling quick

To feed lot or to frying pan,

So much so, deep cisco friends

Might have wondered,

    if they could,

How a population ends,

Evidently gone for good.

As if to help these fish die out,

Humans introduced the eel

Executioners whose snouts

Took a fish apart piecemeal.

In the end, grim sea lampreys

Reaped the harvest hungrily.

Who, adrift those dying days,

Felt a ripple in the sea?

MISS WALDRON'S
RED COLOBUS MONKEY

We searched the trees for you for seven years

In places where you once were thought to be,

But nothing could alleviate our fears,

Except some sign of your mortality.

Your booming voices might create a riot,

Or simply spunky monkey jamborees.

And now in this unsettled peace and quiet,

Blue stamps the sky and mournful soughs the breeze.

Two centuries have passed since we last lost

A primate species to antiquity,

And who on earth could estimate the cost

Of missing branches on the family tree?

Where have you gone, Miss Waldron's Colobus?

What distant destiny? What farther shore?

Your playful screaming echoed silence, thus

You were officially declared . . . *no more.*

Scientists clone pigs in hopes of one day growing
animal organs for human transplants.

2002

Astronomers discover the 91st known planet outside
our solar system; it is 51 light-years away.

ENDNOTES

The Aurochs: Did you ever wonder where all of our modern cattle come from? Angus, Charlois, Guernsey, Holstein. Their great ancestor was the Aurochs, the black bull drawn on cave walls by prehistoric artists. The stuff of many European myths, the Aurochs ranged throughout Europe and Asia but was always hunted for its meat and horns. A royal decree in Poland (c. 1300), where the animal was most prolific, protected it from human slaughter, and local villagers served as its gamekeepers. Still, by 1600, only a handful of these wild oxen remained. Modern efforts at reintroducing the extinct Aurochs by back-breeding have failed.

The Dodo: Called *duodo* ("simpleton") in Portuguese, this slow, flightless, odd-looking bird had only one home—the island of Mauritius in the Indian Ocean. No specimen of the Dodo survives, though its appearance can be approximated from its skeletal remains. Until 1505, the Dodo had never seen a human. But when sailors discovered Mauritius as a convenient stopover on long sea voyages, the Dodo's fate was sealed. Man and the animals he introduced made short work of the species. Within a hundred years of human habitation, the Dodo was a rare bird on the threshold of no more.

Chatham Island Swan: Four hundred fifty miles from any other inhabited land, the group of ten Chatham Islands is a part of New Zealand. Morioris, the first human settlers, populated them in 1000 A.D. The Chatham Island Swan, lovely by being, innocent by nature, defenseless in its habitat, found its way to dinner tables—and to extinction—even before the British colonized the islands in 1791.

The Elephant Bird: Eggs three feet around, larger than the largest dinosaur eggs? Such were the eggs of the flightless Elephant Bird, a species that stood ten or eleven feet tall and weighed over half a ton. (By comparison, a huge ostrich might reach eight feet and three hundred pounds.) The island of Madagascar, off the eastern coast of Africa, was its home, populated first by Africans and Indonesians, then by Muslim traders. By the time Europeans arrived around 1500, the Elephant Bird, the largest ever to have existed on Earth, was already rare, a victim of egg thieves and slaughter.

Steller's Sea Cow: In 1741, Captain Vitus Bering's ship *St. Peter* went down off Kamchatka Island on the far eastern coast of Russia. The Steller's Sea Cow (named after the Bering expedition's naturalist) provided food and clothing for the weary sailors, who returned home safely. Within thirty years, their fellow seamen had hunted the animal to extinction. Members of the same order as manatees and dugongs, sea cows fed on seaweed. As much as twenty-eight feet long, drifting gently just beneath the surface, they were often mistaken for overturned boats. When one cow was harpooned, the females, far from fleeing, surrounded her for protection. Those who managed to escape immediate death by Russian harpoons or rifles were often hit nonetheless and died from their wounds at sea.

The Blue Buck: South Africa's smaller cousin to the roan and sable, the Blue Antelope (bloubok) was never very widespread. Little is known about its behavior. The extinction of the southern African plains zebra, or quagga, in 1883 received much more publicity. When humans made the very gradual shift from hunting and gathering to herding sheep and cattle around two thousand years ago, the Blue Antelope probably suffered at competitive grazing sites. Later, European guns fired the final blow.

Rodriguez Greater Saddleback Tortoise: It is difficult to imagine an animal more defenseless against human predation than the turtle. Now an island outpost of Mauritius in the Indian Ocean, Rodriguez was once home to the Greater Saddleback. One early explorer reported that the tortoises were so abundant a man could walk a hundred paces over their backs without setting foot on the ground. Little is known about their behavior except that they were too readily accessible to seafarers.

The Painted Vulture: Possibly related to the King Vulture, the beautiful Painted Vulture was about the size of a turkey buzzard. After savannah fires, the birds would gather in flocks to feed on "roasted reptiles." It was said (by naturalist William Bartram in the only confirmed sighting in 1791), that "a large portion of [the bird's] stomach hangs down on the breast when it is loaded with food." Why it became extinct is not known for certain, though particularly severe frosts may have been to blame.

The Great Auk: Whether the scene was the Grand Banks, Iceland, or the Faeroe Islands, the Great Auk was killed for sport, taken for food, or bludgeoned for fun. When the world's climate was colder, the species could be found in Italy, Spain, and on America's coasts from Florida to Maine. By the 1820s, the bird in large numbers was a thing of the past. After a particularly severe storm on an island in the New Hebrides in 1844, the island's superstitious natives demanded a scapegoat. An auk was captured, found guilty of witchcraft, and stoned to death by an angry mob. Before and after the bird was gone from the Earth, the trade in rare Great Auk eggs flourished in art museums and private collections.

Eastern Elk (Wapiti): An animal of grace and bearing, the Wapiti was a giant form of the European Red Deer. It was not an elk at all, despite its name. The Eastern Elk was at one time as crucial to the lives of Native Americans (especially the Sioux) as the bison. Prized for its meat and leather, the animal was persecuted mainly for its famous "Elk teeth," which ornamented many Indian robes. Ironically, the fraternal Order of Elks—a charitable organization sponsoring health, veterans, and scholarship programs—used the teeth as watch-chain insignia, refused to accept any substitute, and thereby created a demand that overwhelmed the species. The last Eastern Elk was shot in Pennsylvania on September 1, 1877.

The Quagga: Almost always found in the company of wildebeest, hartebeest, and ostriches, the Quagga was a brown, rather than a striped, zebra with white legs and tail. The Hottentots called it "Quahah" to imitate the animal's shrill, whinnying cry. Restricted in its territory to the Cape Colony and Orange State of South Africa, the animal was hunted relentlessly for its meat. White colonists called the Boers kept tamed Quaggas to guard over their domestic stock, knowing that these high-strung zebras were quick to sound alarm. In the 1830s, these eccentric animals could even be seen in England as coach horses. The destruction of the great herds of the 1840s seems to have taken only about 30 years.

The Laughing Owl: Always in the evening, it was said, after it awoke, the Laughing Owl emitted its plaintive call. Short wings rendered this New Zealand bird a poor flyer but a master at ground hunting. So it was that weasels, introduced to control the rabbit nuisance, found the owls easy prey. After he stuffed the second-to-last Laughing Owl, a female, Thomas Hyatt Potts, the naturalist in question, took a trip to Brisbane. There he bought himself a grandly garish accordion. Upon his return, he would sit in the same spot of his dubious achievement and play to the forest. Occasionally, the last Laughing Owl would sweep over Potts's bald head with laughter or tears. It was difficult to say which.

Arizona Jaguar: The largest cat in the New World, this species was called "big spotted lion" by the Kammei tribe. A forest-dwelling, water-loving cat, the jaguar ranged throughout eastern Arizona north of the Grand Canyon and in southwestern New Mexico. It was said that in the Mohave Desert, Native Americans too old and feeble to hunt for meat used to make a habit of trailing jaguars to dig up edible deer remains buried by the cats. The last documented sightings occurred in New Mexico in 1905.

The Passenger Pigeon: Perhaps never in history has there been a more compelling example of man's power to annihilate another species. No one alive today can remember the awesome spectacle of Passenger Pigeons in flight. When, in the millions, they stopped to rest or roost, tree branches, fat as piano legs, snapped like twigs. A single rifle blast could kill two hundred birds. Pigeons could turn a forest floor into a snowland with bird droppings. In the 1700s, pigeons sold at six birds to the penny, and New England tables groaned with "pigeon pie." Cheap meat, soft pillow feathers, and trap shooters' demands drove the market for these migrating doves to its swift and predictable end.

Carolina Parakeet: As old American forests were cut down to make way for agriculture, this brilliantly plumed songbird lost its habitat and its future. Once upon a time, the birds had found their way into human homes as pets and as feathers for ladies' hats. Having developed a fondness for many kinds of fruits and grains in the southeastern United States, the parakeet was condemned as a pest and subjected to wholesale slaughter. The last wild parakeet was killed in Florida in 1913. Five years later, the one remaining captive bird died at the Cincinnati Zoo.

The Barbary Lion: The European, Tunisian, Algerian, and Cape lions? All are ancient history. Among the largest, the Barbary Lion was the last to go. At a time when Rome was logging in North Africa, the emperors decided to also take this species back to Italy, where the cats would amuse Romans and eat Christians. Once numerous in all North African forests, the heavy-bodied, great-maned Barbary Lion made its last stand in the Atlas Mountains alongside the similarly soon-to-be-extinct Atlas Bear.

Badlands (Audubon's) Bighorn Sheep: Lewis and Clark saw them grazing in the upper Missouri valleys. Now, only their cousins, the Rocky Mountain bighorns, still dot high vistas in the West. The Badlands Bighorn was a victim of its own ingenuity. As settlers moved into its territory, the animal took refuge in the high rock outcrops. But those buttes became isolated islands with little or no food. The sheep could survive neither hunting pressure nor urban encroachment.

Tasmanian Pouched Wolf: It wasn't a wolf or a tiger, a kangaroo, a zebra, or a hyena. A 'possum, perhaps? Like the opossum, it was a marsupial with a backward-opening pouch, but it looked like a canine. Once the Aborigines and their pet dogs (dingoes) arrived in Australia and Tasmania, the Pouched Wolf—or Thylacine, as it was often called—was doomed. Unable to shake its reputation as a killer of livestock, the animal was hunted ruthlessly. Habitat destruction and disease did the rest. In a classic case of government mismanagement, the Thylacine was granted complete protection in 1936, three years after the last one was captured.

Hawaiian O-O: This mysterious honeyeater, native to the Hawaiian paradise, possessed splendid beauty. Restricted to the islands' mountain forests, the birds' yellow feathers were the most desirable plumage for a king's cape or a chief's sarong. Radiance such as theirs pays a price. But apart from their feathered regalia, four of the five Hawaiian O-O species were wiped out largely by cats, rats, and cattle introduced on the islands. The latter's foraging destroyed much of their habitat.

Bali Tiger: In the short space of seventy years, three species of tiger have disappeared—the Caspian, the Javan, and the Bali. The latter's numbers dropped drastically during the two world wars when uncontrolled hunting by Dutch colonials and natives became fashionable. There are no known photographs of the Bali, the smallest of all eight tiger species. The last female was shot in West Bali on September 27, 1937.

Deepwater Cisco: In 1885, in Lake Michigan alone, the salmon-like Deepwater Cisco and its cousin, the blackfin cisco, added fifteen million tons to fishermen's holds. But overharvesting, especially with nets, drastically depleted the species. The fish's end came when humans introduced sea lampreys (eels), which used their sucker-like mouths to fasten themselves onto fish and suck the life out of them. The Deepwater Cisco disappeared at just about the time scientists discovered the chemical TFM, which brought the sea lamprey population under control.

Miss Waldron's Red Colobus Monkey: It has been two hundred years (1800) since a primate met its end. But say good-bye to a near relative. This large and conspicuous monkey recently was declared extinct. And it was not for want of prime monkey habitat. Chalk up its disappearance to hunting and inadequate government protection. By 2000, a Red Colobus had not been seen in the West African rain forest for at least twenty years. Researchers are certain of this: They listened long for its high-pitched howl, but all they heard was silence.